THE COMPLETE ORGAN PL
HYMN BOOK

Wise Publications
London/New York/Sydney

Exclusive Distributors:
Music Sales Limited
8/9 Frith Street, London W1V 5TZ, England.
Music Sales Pty, Limited
120 Rothschild Avenue, Rosebery, NSW 2018, Australia.

This book © Copyright 1984 by
Wise Publications
UK ISBN 0.7119.0565.7
UK Order No. AM 37680

Designed by Howard Brown

Music Sales' complete catalogue lists thousands of
titles and is free from your local music shop,
or direct from Music Sales Limited.
Please send £1.50 Cheque or Postal Order for postage to
Music Sales Limited, 8/9 Frith Street, London W1V 5TZ.

Printed in England by
Caligraving Limited, Thetford, Norfolk.

CONTENTS

HYMN CATEGORY INDEX

O WORSHIP THE KING

Traditional

Registration No ⑥
Suggested Drum Rhythm: **Waltz**

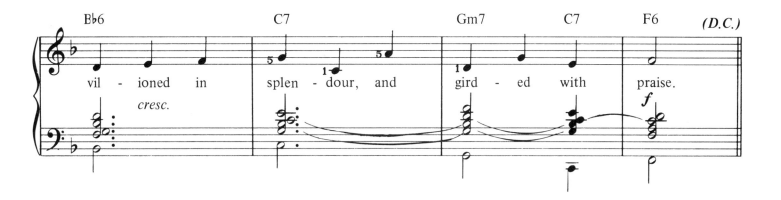

vil - ioned in splen - dour, and gird - ed with praise.

2. O tell of His might, O sing of His grace,
   Whose robe is the light, Whose canopy space;
   His chariots of wrath the deep thunder clouds form,
   And dark is His path on the wings of the storm.

3. The earth with its store of wonders untold,
   Almighty, Thy power hath founded of old;
   Hath 'stablished it fast by a changeless decree,
   And round it hath cast, like a mantle, the sea.

4. Thy bountiful care what tongue can recite?
   It breathes in the air, it shines in the light;
   It streams from the hills, it descends to the plain,
   And sweetly distils in the dew and the rain.

5. Frail children of dust and feeble as frail,
   In Thee do we trust, nor find Thee to fail;
   Thy mercies how tender, how firm to the end,
   Our Maker, Defender, Redeemer and Friend.

6. O measureless Might, ineffable Love,
   While angels delight to hymn Thee above,
   Thy humbler creation, though feeble their lays,
   With true adoration shall sing to Thy praise.

O GOD OUR HELP

Traditional

Registration No ②
Suggested Drum Rhythm: **Bossa Nova**

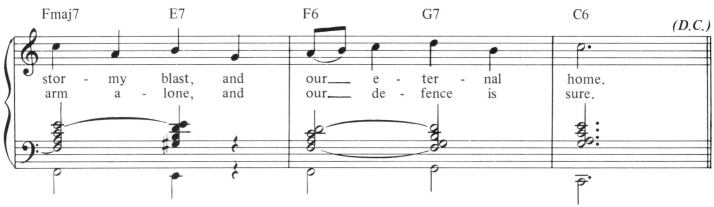

3. Before the hills in order stood,
   Or earth received her frame,
   From everlasting Thou art God,
   To endless years the same.

4. A thousand ages in Thy sight
   Are like an evening gone,
   Short as the watch that ends the night
   Before the rising sun.

5. Time, like an ever-rolling stream,
   Bears all its sons away,
   They fly forgotten, as a dream
   Dies at the opening day.

6. O God our help in ages past,
   Our hope for years to come,
   Be Thou our guard while troubles last,
   And our eternal home.

THE LORD'S MY SHEPHERD

Traditional

Registration No ④
Suggested Drum Rhythm: **Waltz**

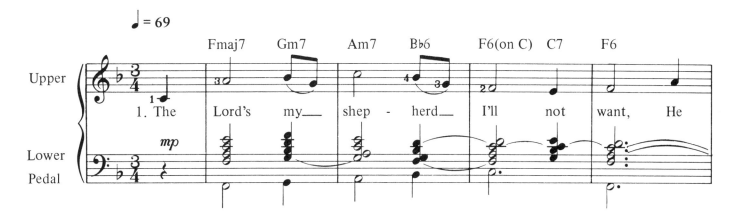

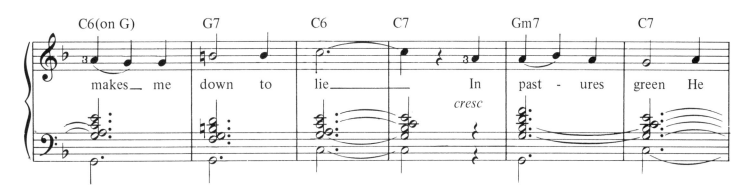

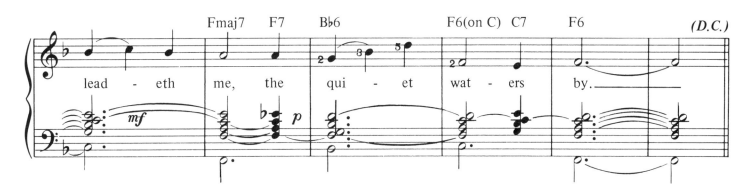

2. My soul He doth restore again,
And me to walk doth make,
Within the paths of righteousness,
E'en for His own name's sake.

3. Yea, though I walk in death's dark vale,
Yet will I fear none ill;
For Thou art with me and Thy rod
And staff me comfort still.

4. The table Thou hast furnished
In presence of my foes;
My head Thou dost with oil anoint,
And my cup overflows.

5. Goodness and mercy all my life
Shall surely follow me;
And in God's house for evermore
My dwelling-place shall be.

ALL PEOPLE THAT ON EARTH DO DWELL

Traditional

Registration No ① 1
Suggested Drum Rhythm: **Swing**

2. The Lord, ye know, is God indeed;
   Without our aid He did us make;
   We are His folk, He doth us feed,
   And for His sheep He doth us take.

3. O enter then His gates with praise,
   Approach with joy His courts unto:
   Praise, laud and bless His name always,
   For it is seemly so to do.

4. For why? the Lord our God is good;
   His mercy is for ever sure:
   His truth at all times firmly stood,
   And shall from age to age endure.

5. To Father, Son, and Holy Ghost,
   The God whom heaven and earth adore,
   From men and from the angel-host
   Be praise and glory evermore.

PRAISE TO THE HOLIEST

Traditional

Registration No ⑤
Suggested Drum Rhythm: **Waltz**

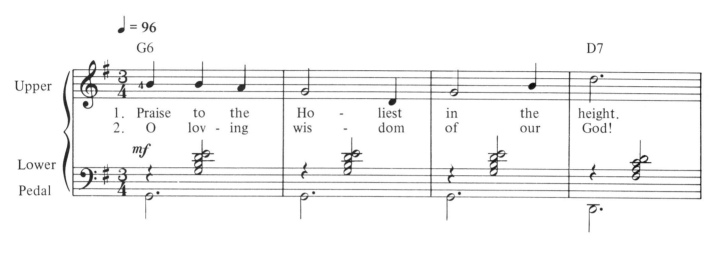

1. Praise to the Ho - liest in the height.
2. O lov - ing wis - dom of our God!

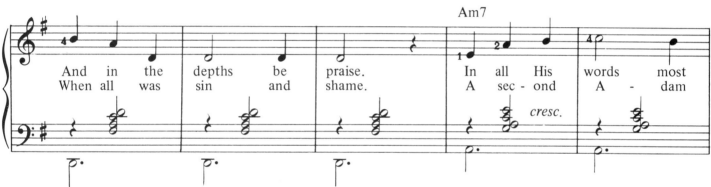

And in the depths be praise. In all His words most
When all was sin and shame. A sec - ond A - dam

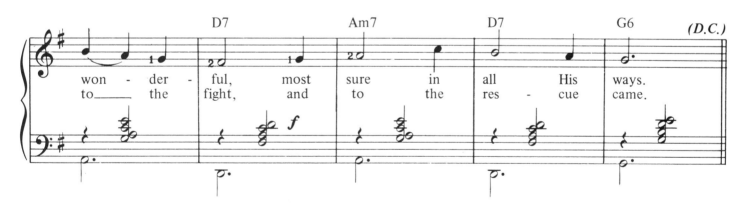

won - der - ful, most sure in all His ways.
to the fight, most and to the res - cue came.

(D.C.)

3. O wisest love! that flesh and blood,
   Which did in Adam fail;
   Should strive afresh against the foe,
   Should strive and should prevail.

4. And that a higher gift than grace
   Should flesh and blood refine,
   God's presence and His very self,
   And essence all-divine.

5. O generous love! that he who smote
   In Man for man the foe,
   The double agony in Man
   For man should undergo.

6. And in the garden secretly,
   And on the cross on high,
   Should teach His brethren and inspire
   To suffer and to die.

9

JERUSALEM THE GOLDEN

Traditional

Registration No ③
Suggested Drum Rhythm: **Swing**

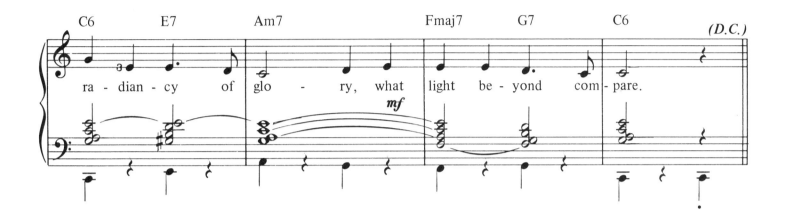

2. They stand, those halls of Zion,
   Conjubilant with song,
   And bright with many an angel
   And all the martyr throng;
   The Prince is ever in them,
   The daylight is serene,
   The pastures of the blessed
   Are decked in glorious sheen.

3. There is the throne of David,
   And there from care released,
   The shout of them that triumph,
   The song of them that feast;
   And they who, with their Leader,
   Have conquered in the fight,
   For ever and for ever
   Are clad in robes of white.

4. Jerusalem the glorious,
   The home of God's elect;
   O dear and future vision
   That eager hearts expect.
   Jesu, in mercy bring us
   To that dear land of rest,
   Who art, with God the Father,
   And Spirit, ever blest.

PRAISE MY SOUL THE KING OF HEAVEN

Traditional

Registration No 7
Suggested Drum Rhythm: **March** 2/4 **(or Swing)**

CHORUS

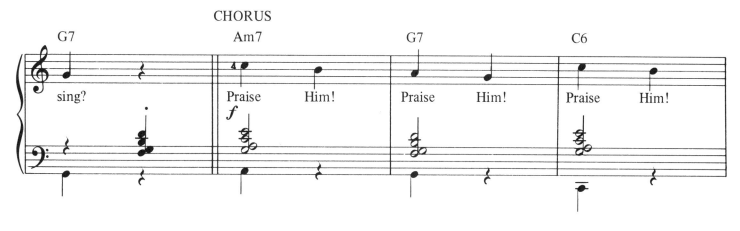

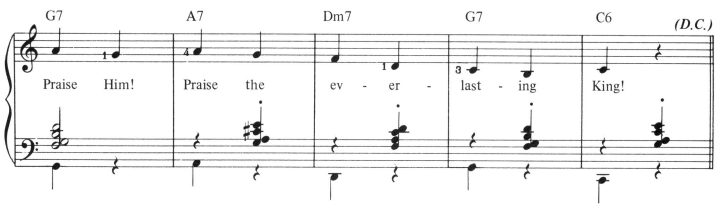

2. Praise Him for His grace and favour
   To our fathers in distress;
   Praise Him still the same for ever,
   Slow to chide and swift to bless;
   Praise Him! praise Him!
   Praise Him! praise Him!
   Glorious in His faithfulness.

3. Father-like He tends and spares us;
   Well our feeble frame He knows;
   In His hands He gently bears us,
   Rescues us from all our foes:
   Praise Him! praise Him!
   Praise Him! praise Him!
   Widely as His mercy flows!

4. Frail as summer's flower we flourish,
   Blows the wind and it is gone;
   But while mortals rise and perish
   God endures unchanging on.
   Praise Him! praise Him!
   Praise Him! praise Him!
   Praise the High Eternal One.

5. Angels, help us to adore Him,
   Ye behold Him face to face;
   Sun and moon, bow down before Him,
   Dwellers all in time and space:
   Praise Him! praise Him!
   Praise Him! praise Him!
   Praise with us the God of grace!

NOW THANK WE ALL OUR GOD

Traditional

Registration No ⑧
Suggested Drum Rhythm: **Swing**

2. O may this bounteous God
   Through all our life be near us,
   With ever joyful hearts
   And blessed peace to cheer us;
   And keep us in His grace,
   And guide us when perplexed,
   And free us from all ills
   In this world and the next.

3. All praise and thanks to God
   The Father now be given,
   The Son and Him who reigns
   With them in highest heaven;
   The one eternal God,
   Whom earth and heaven adore,
   For this it was, is now,
   And shall be evermore.

HOLY, HOLY, HOLY

Traditional

Registration No ③
Suggested Drum Rhythm: **Swing**

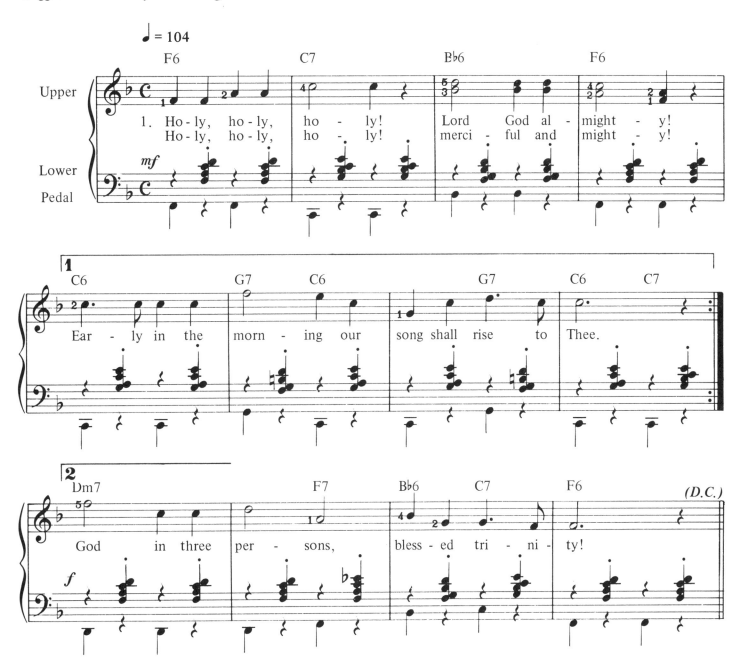

2. Holy, holy, holy! All the saints adore Thee,
Casting down their golden crowns around the
glassy sea,
Cherubim and seraphim, falling down before Thee,
Who wert and art, and evermore shalt be.

3. Holy, holy. holy! Though the darkness hide Thee,
Though the eye of sinful man Thy glory may not
see,
Only Thou art holy, there is none beside Thee
Perfect in power, in love and purity.

4. Holy, holy, holy! Lord God Almighty!
All Thy works shall praise Thy name, in earth and
sky and sea:
Holy, holy, holy! Merciful and mighty.
God in three Persons, blessed trinity.

THE DAY THOU GAVEST LORD IS ENDED

Traditional

Registration No ① 1
Suggested Drum Rhythm: **Waltz**

♩ = 92

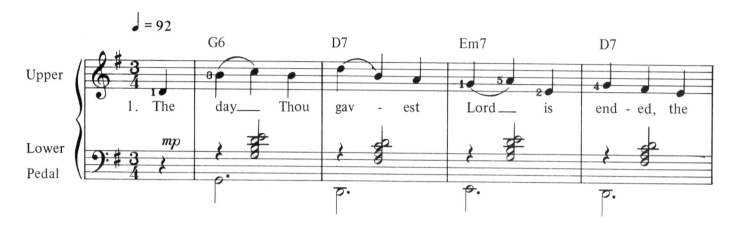

1. The day__ Thou gav - est Lord__ is end - ed, the

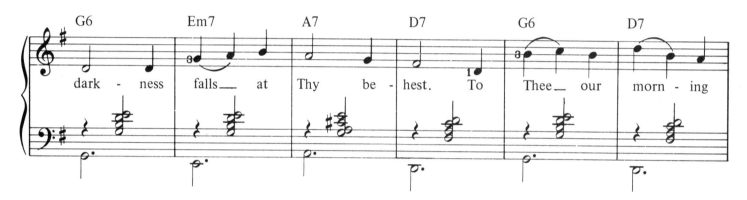

dark - ness falls__ at Thy be - hest. To Thee__ our morn - ing

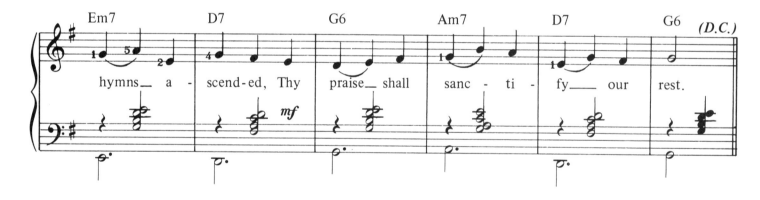

hymns__ a - scend-ed, Thy praise__ shall sanc - ti - fy__ our rest. *(D.C.)*

2. We thank Thee that Thy church unsleeping,
   While earth rolls onward into light,
   Through all the world her watch is keeping,
   And rests not now by day or night.

3. As o'er each continent and island
   The dawn leads on to another day,
   The voice of prayer is never silent,
   Nor dies the strain of praise away.

4. The sun that bids us rest is waking
   Our brethren 'neath the western sky,
   And hour by hour fresh lips are making
   Thy wondrous doings heard on high.

5. So be it, Lord: Thy throne shall never
   Like earth's proud empires, pass away;
   Thy kingdom stands and grows forever
   Till all Thy creatures own Thy sway.

THROUGH THE NIGHT OF DOUBT AND SORROW

Traditional

Registration No ④
Suggested Drum Rhythm: **Swing**

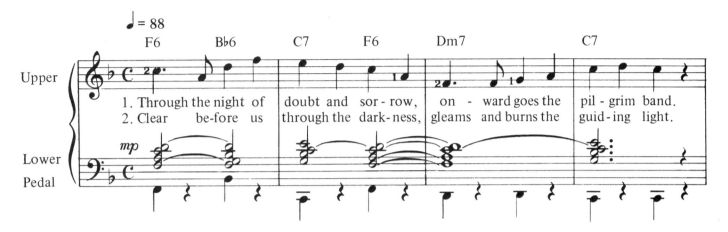

1. Through the night of doubt and sor-row, on-ward goes the pil-grim band.
2. Clear be-fore us through the dark-ness, gleams and burns the guid-ing light.

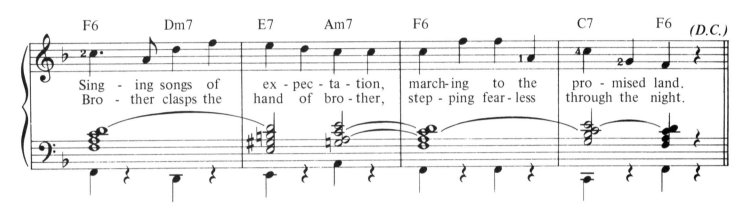

Sing-ing songs of ex-pec-ta-tion, march-ing to the pro-mised land.
Bro-ther clasps the hand of bro-ther, step-ping fear-less through the night.

(D.C.)

3. One the light of God's own presence
   O'er His ransomed people shed.
   Chasing far the gloom and terror,
   Brightening all the path we tread.

4. One the object of our journey,
   One the faith which never tires,
   One the earnest looking forward,
   One the hope our God inspires.

5. One the strain that lips of thousands
   Lift as from the heart of one.
   One the conflict, one the peril,
   One the march in God begun.

6. One the gladness of rejoicing
   On the far eternal shore,
   Where the One Almighty Father
   Reigns in love for evermore.

7. Onward, therefore, pilgrim brothers,
   Onward with the Cross our aid;
   Bear its shame and fight its battle,
   Till we rest beneath its shade.

8. Soon shall come the great awaking,
   Soon the rending of the tomb;
   Then the scattering of all shadows,
   And the end of toil and gloom.

ROCK OF AGES

Traditional

Registration No ①
Suggested Drum Rhythm: **Waltz**

3. Nothing in my hand I bring,
   Simply to Thy cross I cling;
   Naked, come to Thee for dress:
   Helpless, look to Thee for grace;
   Foul, I to the fountain fly;
   Wash me, Saviour, or I die.

4. While I draw this fleeting breath,
   When mine eyes shall close in death,
   When I soar through tracts unknown,
   See Thee on Thy judgement throne,
   Rock of ages, cleft for me,
   Let me hide myself in Thee.

HE WHO WOULD VALIANT BE

Traditional

Registration No (7)
Suggested Drum Rhythm: **Swing**

2. Who so beset him round
   With dismal stories,
   Do but themselves confound:
   His strength the more is.
   No foes shall stay his might,
   Though he with giants fight,
   He will make good his right
   To be a pilgrim.

3. Since, Lord, Thou dost defend
   Us with Thy Spirit,
   We know we at the end
   Shall life inherit.
   Then fancies flee away!
   I'll fear not what men say,
   I'll labour night and day
   To be a pilgrim.

THE OLD RUGGED CROSS

Traditional

Registration No ②
Suggested Drum Rhythm: **Waltz**

3. In the old rugged cross, stained with love so
                divine,
  A wondrous beauty I see;
  For t'was on that old cross Jesus suffered and
                died
  To pardon and sanctify me.
    So I'll cherish (etc.)

4. To the old rugged cross, I will ever be true,
  Its shame and reproach gladly bear;
  Then He'll call me some day to my home far
                away,
  Where His glory for ever I'll share.
    So I'll cherish (etc.)

THERE IS A GREEN HILL FAR AWAY

Traditional

Registration No ④
Suggested Drum Rhythm: **Bossa Nova**

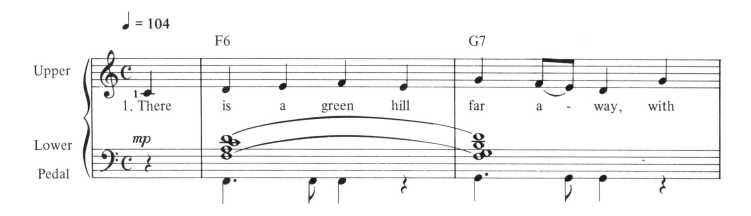

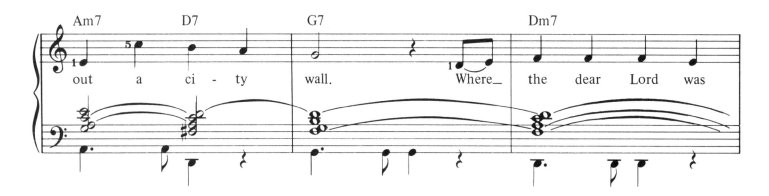

2. We may not know, we cannot tell,
   What pains He had to bear,
   But we believe it was for us
   He hung and suffered there.

3. He died that we might be forgiven,
   He died to make us good;
   That we might go at last to Heaven,
   Saved by His precious blood.

4. There was no other good enough
   To pay the price of sin;
   He only could unlock the gate
   Of Heaven, and let us in.

5. O dearly, dearly has He loved,
   And we must love Him too,
   And trust in His redeeming blood,
   And try His works to do.

HOW SWEET THE NAME OF JESUS SOUNDS

Traditional

Registration No ③
Suggested Drum Rhythm: **Cha-cha**

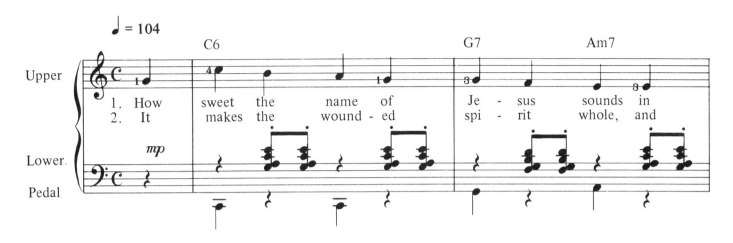

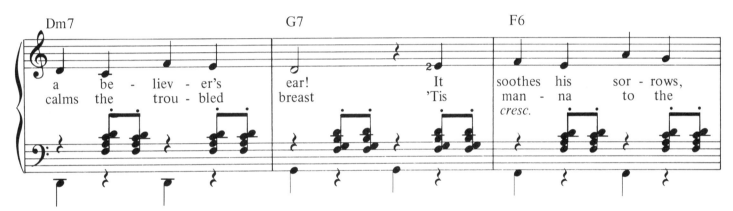

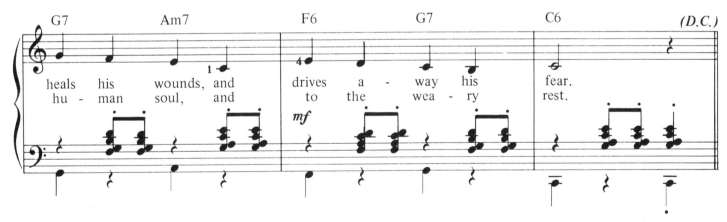

3. Dear name! the rock on which I build,
My shield and hiding place,
My never-failing treasury filled
With boundless stores of grace.

4. Jesus! my Shepherd, Brother, Friend,
My Prophet, Priest and King,
My Lord, my Life, my Way, my End,
Accept the praise I bring.

5. Weak is the effort of my heart,
And cold my warmest thought;
But when I see Thee as Thou art,
I'll praise Thee as I ought.

6. Till then I would Thy love proclaim
With ev'ry fleeting breath;
And may the music of Thy name
Refresh my soul in death.

WHEN I SURVEY THE WONDROUS CROSS

Traditional

Registration No ②
Suggested Drum Rhythm: **Waltz**

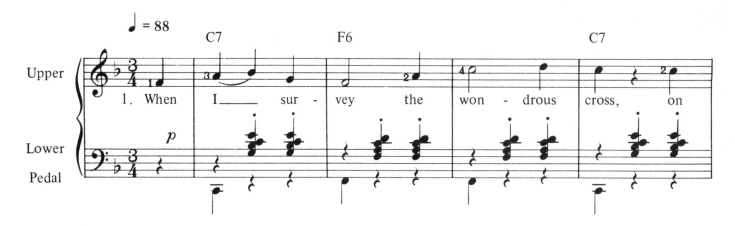

1. When I____ sur - vey the won - drous cross, on

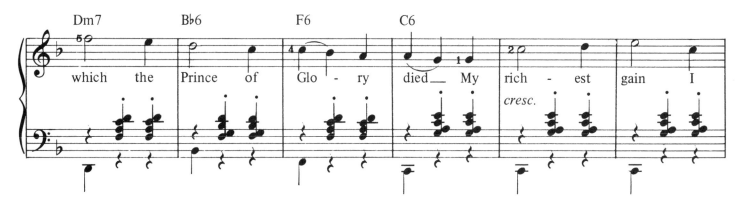

which the Prince of Glo - ry died____ My rich - est gain I

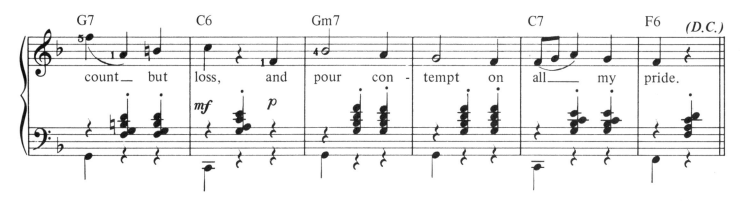

count____ but loss, and pour con - tempt on all____ my pride. *(D.C.)*

2. Forbid it Lord, that I should boast,
   Save in the death of Christ, my God;
   All the vain things that charm me most,
   I sacrifice them to His blood.

3. See from His head, His hands, His feet
   Sorrow and love flow mingled down;
   Did e'er such love and sorrow meet,
   Or thorns compose so rich a crown?

4. His dying crimson, like a robe,
   Spreads o'er His body on the tree;
   Then am I dead to all the globe,
   And all the globe is dead to me.

5. Were the whole realm of nature mine,
   That were a present far too small;
   Love so amazing, so divine,
   Demands my soul, my life, my all.

LEAD KINDLY LIGHT

Traditional

Registration No ④
Suggested Drum Rhythm: **Bossa Nova**

(D.C.)

2. I was not ever thus, nor prayed that Thou
   Should'st lead me on,
   I loved to choose and see my path, but now
   Lead Thou me on.
   I loved the garish day, and spite of fears,
   Pride ruled my will; remember not past years.

3. So long Thy power hath blessed me, sure it still
   Will lead me on,
   O'er moor and fen, o'er crag and torrent, till
   The night is gone;
   And with the morn those angel faces smile
   Which I have loved long since, and lost awhile.

ALL THINGS BRIGHT AND BEAUTIFUL

Traditional

Registration No ⑤
Suggested Drum Rhythm: **Swing**

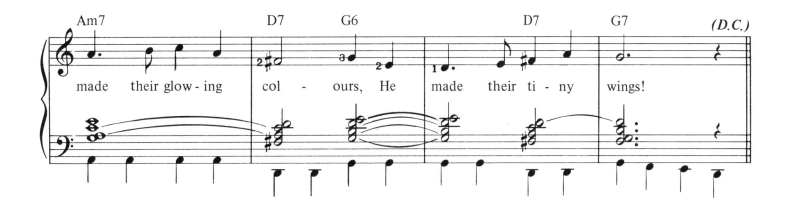

2. The purple headed mountain,
   The river running by;
   The sunset and the morning
   That brightens up the sky;
       All things bright (etc.)

3. The cold wind in the winter,
   The pleasant summer sun,
   The ripe fruits in the garden,
   He made them ev'ry one:
       All things bright (etc.)

4. The tall trees in the greenwood,
   The meadows where we play,
   The rushes by the water
   We gather ev'ry day:
       All things bright (etc.)

5. He gave us eyes to see them,
   And lips that we might tell
   How great is God Almighty,
   Who has made all things well:
       All things bright (etc.)

NEARER MY GOD TO THEE

Traditional

Registration No ⑧
Suggested Drum Rhythm: **Waltz**

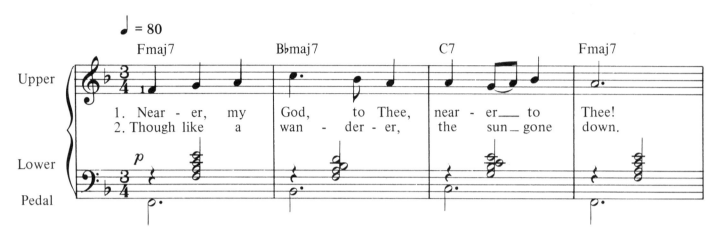

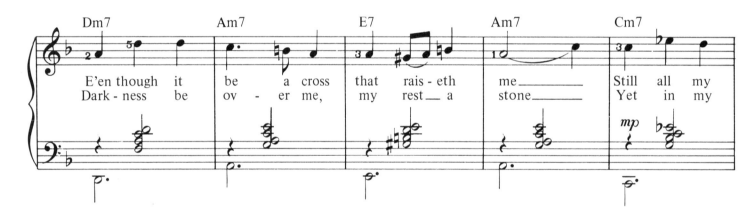

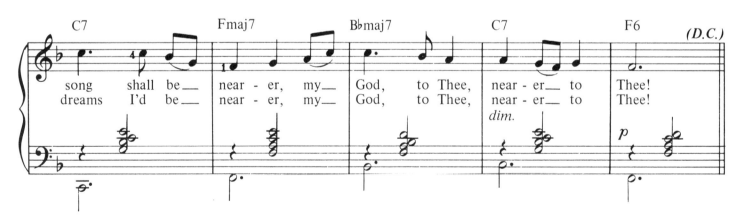

3. There let the way appear,
Steps unto heaven;
All that Thou sendest me
In mercy given:
Angels to beckon me
Nearer, my God, to Thee,
Nearer to Thee!

4. Then, with my waking thoughts
Bright with thy praise,
Out of my stony griefs,
Bethel I'll raise;
So by my woes to be
Nearer, my God, to Thee,
Nearer to Thee!

5. Or if on joyful wing
Cleaving the sky,
Sun, moon and stars forgot,
Upwards I fly;
Still all my song shall be,
Nearer, my God, to Thee,
Nearer to Thee!

THE KING OF LOVE MY SHEPHERD IS

Traditional

Registration No ⑥
Suggested Drum Rhythm: **Cha-cha**

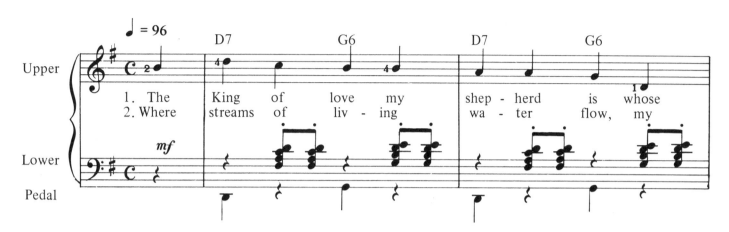

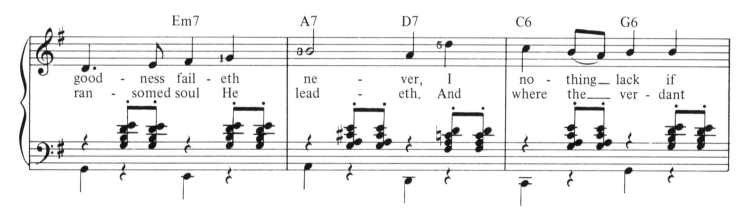

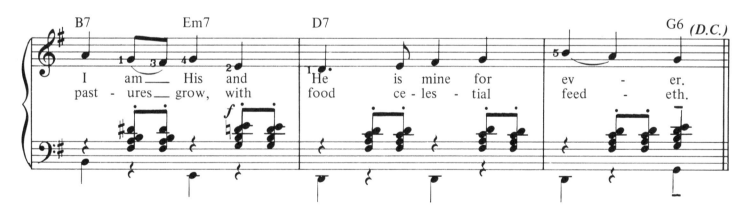

3. Perverse and foolish oft I strayed,
   But yet in love He sought me,
   And on His shoulder gently laid,
   And home rejoicing brought me.

4. In death's dark vale I fear no ill
   With Thee, dear Lord, beside me:
   Thy rod and staff my comfort still,
   Thy cross before to guide me.

5. Thou spread'st a table in my sight;
   Thy unction grace bestoweth;
   And O what transport of delight
   From Thy pure chalice floweth!

6. And so through all the length of days
   Thy goodness faileth never:
   Good Shepherd, may I sing Thy praise
   Within Thy house for ever.

STAND UP, STAND UP FOR JESUS

Traditional

Registration No (7)

Suggested Drum Rhythm: **March** 2/4 (or Swing)

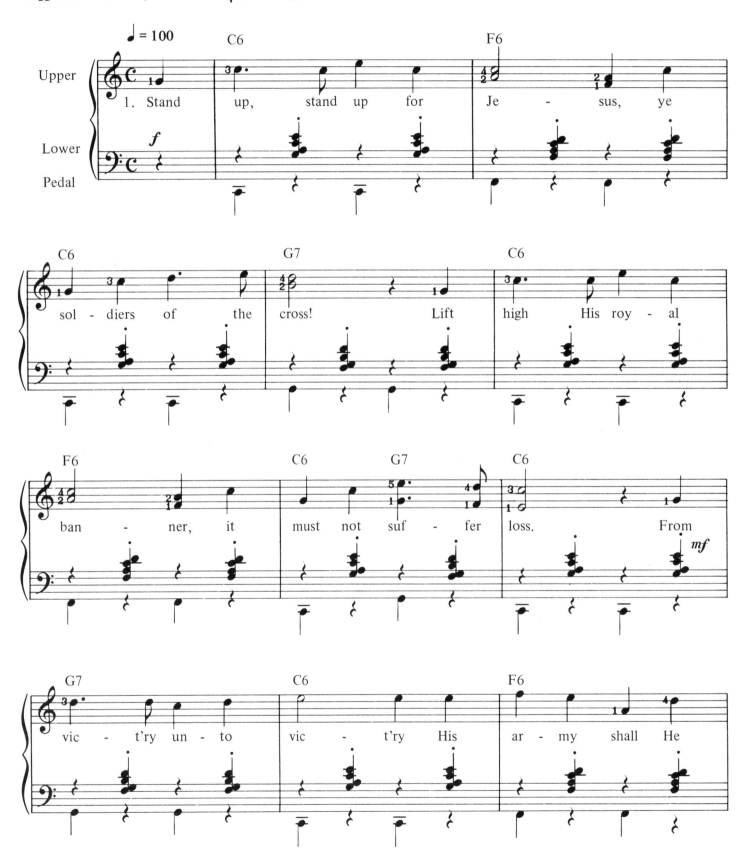

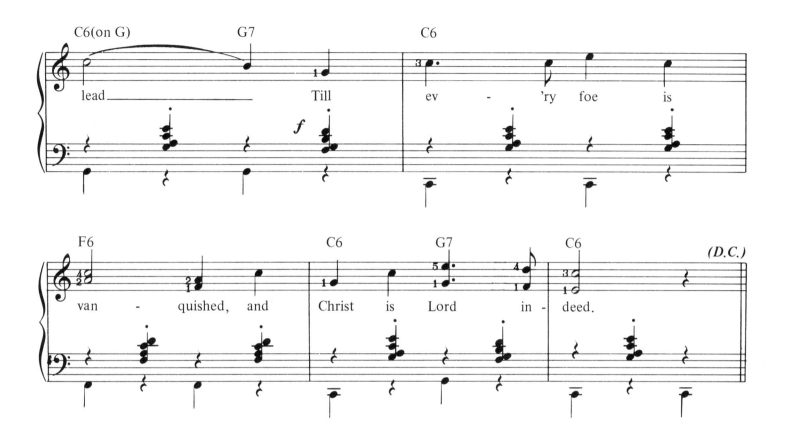

2. Stand up, stand up for Jesus,
   The trumpet call obey;
   Forth to the mighty conflict
   In this His glorious day.
   Ye that are men now serve Him
   Against unnumbered foes;
   Your courage rise with danger,
   And strength to strength oppose.

3. Stand up, stand up for Jesus!
   Stand in His strength alone;
   The arm of flesh will fail you,
   Ye dare not trust your own.
   Put on the gospel armour,
   Each piece put on with prayer:
   Where duty calls or danger,
   Be never wanting there.

4. Stand up, stand up for Jesus!
   Each soldier to his post;
   Close up the broken column
   And shout through all the host.
   Make good the loss so heavy
   In those that still remain;
   And prove to all around you
   That death itself is gain.

5. Stand up, stand up for Jesus!
   The strife will not be long;
   This day the noise of battle,
   The next the victor's song.
   To him that overcometh
   A crown of life shall be:
   He with the King of Glory
   Shall reign eternally.

LEAD US HEAVENLY FATHER

Traditional

Registration No ⑤
Suggested Drum Rhythm: **Bossa Nova**

2. Saviour, breathe forgiveness o'er us;
All our weakness Thou dost know,
Thou didst tread this earth before us,
Thou didst feel its keenest woe;
Lone and dreary, faint and weary,
Through the desert Thou didst go.

3. Spirit of our God, descending,
Fill our hearts with heavenly joy,
Love with every passion blending,
Pleasure that can never cloy:
Thus provided, pardoned, guided,
Nothing can our peace destroy.

AS WITH GLADNESS MEN OF OLD

Traditional

Registration No ⑧
Suggested Drum Rhythm: **Rock**

2. As with joyful steps they sped
   To that lowly manger bed,
   There to bend the knee before
   Him whom heav'n and earth adore:
   So may we with willing feet
   Ever seek Thy mercy seat.

3. As they offered gifts most rare
   At that manger, rude and bare,
   So may we with holy joy,
   Pure, and free from sin's alloy,
   All our costliest treasures bring,
   Christ, to Thee, our heavenly King.

4. Holy Jesus, every day
   Keep us in the narrow way;
   And, when earthly things are past,
   Bring our ransomed souls at last
   Where they need no star to guide,
   Where no clouds Thy glory hide.

5. In the heav'nly country bright
   Need they no created light:
   Thou its light, its joy, its crown,
   Thou its sun which goes not down:
   There for ever may we sing
   Alleluias to our King.

THE CHURCH'S ONE FOUNDATION

Traditional

Registration No 6
Suggested Drum Rhythm: **Cha-cha**

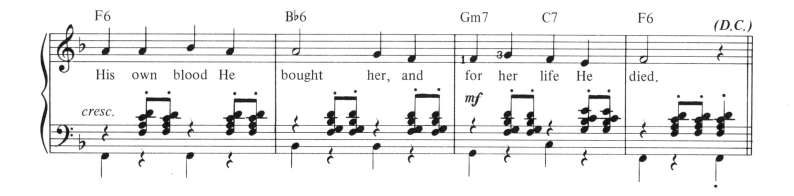

His own blood He bought her, and for her life He died.

2. Elect from ev'ry nation,
   Yet one from all the earth;
   Her charter of salvation
   One Lord, one faith, one birth;
   One holy name she blesses,
   Partakes one holy food,
   And to one hope she presses
   With ev'ry grace endued.

3. Though with a scornful wonder
   Men see her sore oppressed,
   By schisms rent asunder,
   By heresies distressed,
   Yet saints their watch are keeping,
   Their cry goes up "How long?"
   And soon the night of weeping
   Shall be the morn of song.

4. 'Mid toil and tribulation,
   And tumult of her war,
   She waits the consummation
   Of peace for evermore;
   Till with the vision glorious
   Her longing eyes are blest,
   And the great Church victorious
   Shall be the Church at rest.

5. Yet she on earth hath union
   With God the Three in One
   And mystic sweet communion
   With those whose rest is won:
   O happy ones and holy!
   Lord give us grace that we
   Like them, the meek and lowly,
   On high may dwell with Thee.

MINE EYES HAVE SEEN THE GLORY

Traditional

Registration No ⑦
Suggested Drum Rhythm: **March ²⁄₄ (or Swing)**

2. I've seen Him in the watch-fires
   Of a hundred circling camps,
   They have builded Him an altar
   In the evening dews and damps:
   I have read His righteous sentence
   By the dim and flaring lamps,
   His day is marching on.
       Glory, glory Hallelujah! etc.

3. I have read a fiery gospel
   Writ in burnished rows of steel,
   "As ye deal with My contemner,
   So with you My grace shall deal".
   Let the hero born of woman
   Crush the serpent with His heel,
   Since God is marching on.
       Glory, glory, Hallelujah! etc.

4. He hath sounded forth the trumpet
   That shall never call retreat;
   He is sifting out the hearts of men
   Before His judgement seat;
   O, be swift, my soul, to answer Him:
   Be jubilant, my feet!
   Our God is marching on.
       Glory, glory, Hallelujah! etc.

5. In the beauty of the lilies
   Christ was born, across the sea,
   With a glory in His bosom
   That transfigures you and me;
   As He died to make men holy,
   Let us live to make men free,
   While God is marching on.
       Glory, glory, Hallelujah! etc.

TELL ME THE OLD, OLD STORY

Traditional

Registration No (5)
Suggested Drum Rhythm: **March** $\frac{2}{4}$ **(or Swing)**

2. Tell me the story slowly,
 That I may take it in,
 That wonderful redemption,
 God's remedy for sin.
 Tell me the story often,
 For I forget so soon;
 The "early dew" of morning
 Has passed away at noon.
  Tell me the old, old story etc.

3. Tell me the story softly,
 With earnest tones and grave;
 Remember, I'm the sinner
 Whom Jesus came to save.
 Tell me the story always,
 If you would really be,
 In any time of trouble
 A comforter to me.
  Tell me the old, old story etc.

4. Tell me the same old story,
 When you have cause to fear,
 That this world's empty glory
 Is costing me too dear:
 Yes, and when that world's glory
 Is dawning on my soul,
 Tell me the old, old story:
 "Christ Jesus makes thee whole".
  Tell me the old, old story etc.

ETERNAL FATHER STRONG TO SAVE

Traditional

Registration No ③
Suggested Drum Rhythm: **Rock**

3. O sacred Spirit, who didst brood
   Upon the waters dark and rude,
   And bid their angry tumult cease,
   And give, for wild confusion, peace:
   O hear us when we cry to Thee
   For those in peril on the sea.

4. O Trinity of love and power
   Our brethren shield in danger's hour;
   From rock and tempest, fire and foe,
   Protect them wheresoe'er they go;
   And ever let there rise to Thee
   Glad hymns of praise from land and sea.

ABIDE WITH ME

Traditional

Registration No ① 1

Suggested Drum Rhythm: **Bossa Nova**

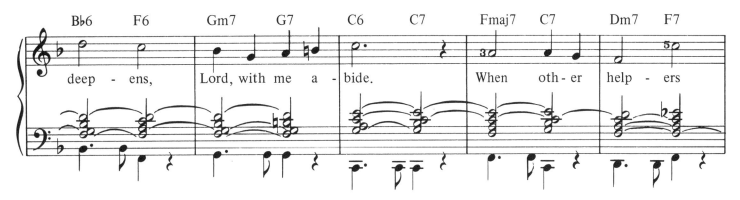

2. Swift to its close ebbs out life's little day;
Earth's joys grow dim, its glories pass away.
Change and decay in all around I see:
O Thou who changest not, abide with me.

3. I need Thy presence ev'ry passing hour;
What but Thy grace can foil the tempter's power?
Who like Thyself my guide and stay can be?
Through cloud and sunshine, O abide with me.

4. I fear no foe, with Thee at hand to bless;
Ills have no weight and tears no bitterness:
Where is death's sting? where, grave, thy victory?
I triumph still if Thou abide with me.

5. Hold Thou Thy cross before my closing eyes,
Shine through the gloom and point me to the
skies;
Heaven's morning breaks and earth's vain shadows
flee:
In life, in death, O Lord, abide with me.

WE PLOUGH THE FIELDS AND SCATTER

Traditional

Registration No ⑥
Suggested Drum Rhythm: **Cha-cha**

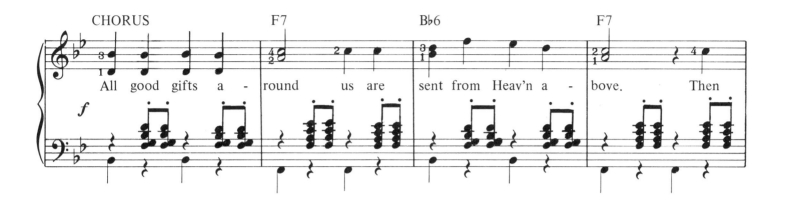

All good gifts a - round us are sent from Heav'n a - bove. Then

thank the Lord, O thank the Lord, for all_____ His love.

(D.C.)

2. He only is the maker
     Of all things near and far,
     He paints the wayside flower,
     He lights the evening star.
     The winds and waves obey Him,
     By Him the birds are fed;
     Much more to us, His children,
     He gives our daily bread.
               All good gifts, etc.

3. We thank Thee then, O Father,
     For all things bright and good;
     The seed-time and the harvest,
     Our life, our health, our food.
     No gifts have we to offer
     For all Thy love imparts,
     But that which Thou desirest,
     Our humble, thankful hearts.
               All good gifts, etc.

ONWARD CHRISTIAN SOLDIERS

Traditional

Registration No ⑧
Suggested Drum Rhythm: **Rock**

2. At the name of Jesus Satan's Host doth flee,
   On then, Christian Soldiers, on to victory:
   Hell's foundations quiver at the shout of praise;
   Brothers, lift your voices, loud your anthems raise.
   Onward Christian Soldiers, *etc.*

3. Like a mighty army moves the Church of God.
   Brothers, we are treading where the saints have trod.
   We are not divided, all one body we,
   One in hope and purpose, one in charity.
   Onward Christian Soldiers, *etc.*

4. Crowns and thrones may perish, kingdoms rise and wane,
   But the Church of Jesus constant will remain:
   Gates of hell can never 'gainst that Church prevail;
   We have Christ's own promise and that cannot fail.
   Onward Christian Soldiers, *etc.*

5. Onward, then, ye people, join our happy throng,
   Blend with ours your voices in the triumph song;
   "Glory, praise and honour unto Christ the King!"
   This through countless ages men and angels sing.
   Onward Christian Soldiers, *etc.*

CHORD CHARTS (For Left Hand)

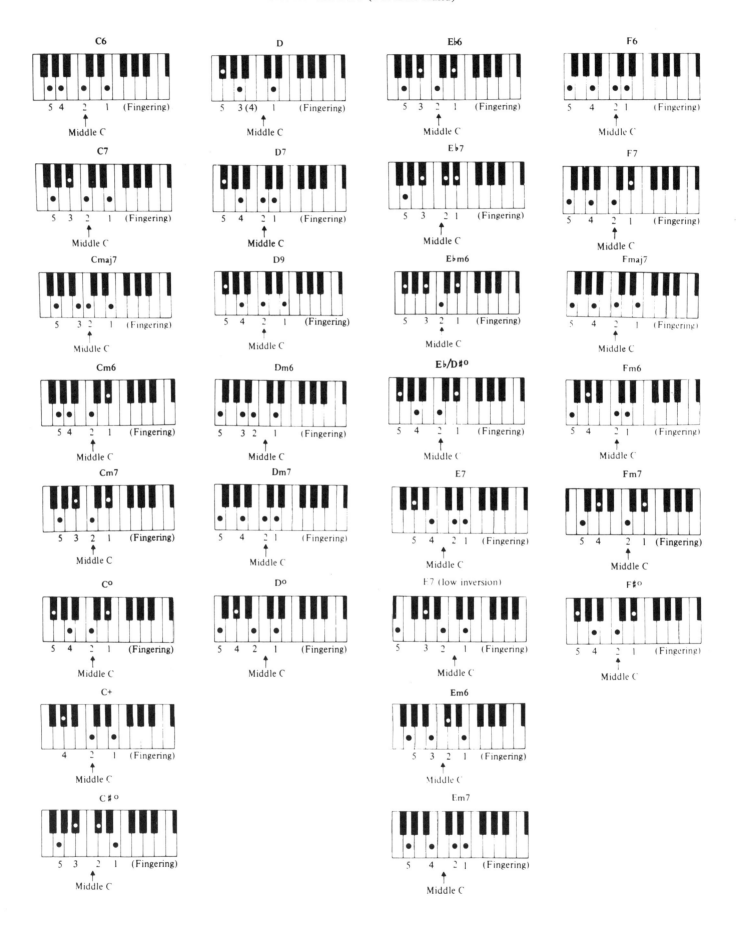

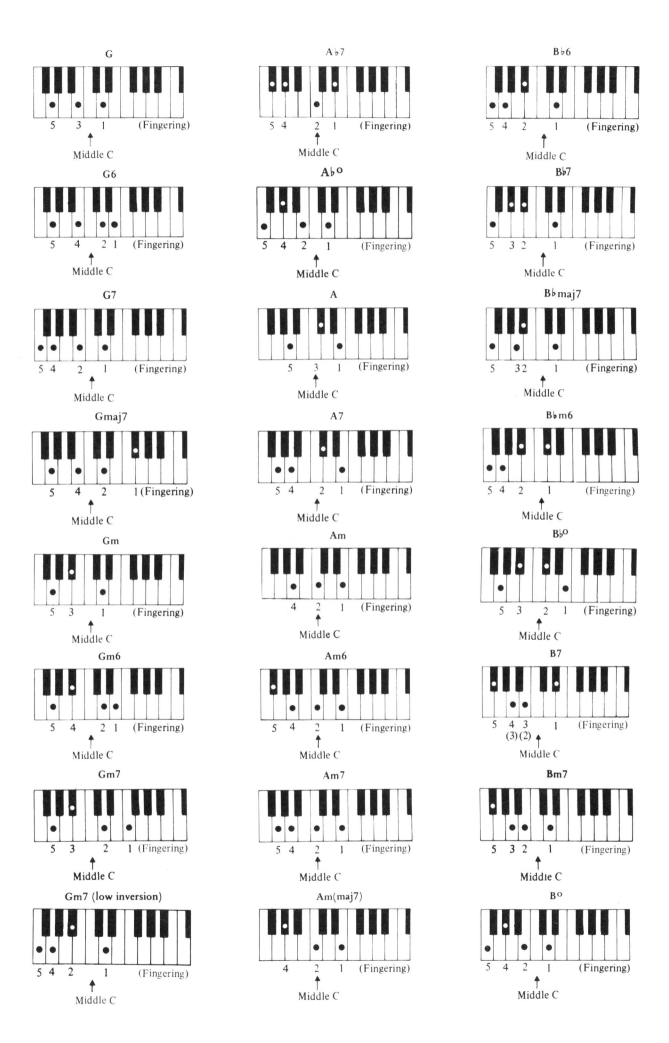

REGISTRATION TABLE
(For All Organs)

GENERAL ELECTRONIC ORGANS	DRAWBAR ORGANS

① Upper: Violin 8'
  Lower: Flutes 8', 4'
  Pedal: 8'
  Vibrato: On (+ delay if available)

① Upper: 00 5666 654
  Lower: (00)6503 000(0)
  Pedal: 4 – (2)
  Vibrato: On (+ delay if available)

② Upper: Oboe 8'
  Lower: Flute 8'
  Pedal: 8'
  Vibrato: On

② Upper: 00 4763 000
  Lower: (00)4404 000(0)
  Pedal: 4 – (2)
  Vibrato: On

③ Upper: Accordion (or Reed 8')
  Lower: Flutes 8', 4'
  Pedal: 8'
  Vibrato: Off. Leslie: Chorale

③ Upper: 00 8866 666
  Lower: (00)8804 000(0)
  Pedal: 5 – (3)
  Vibrato: Off. Leslie: Chorale

④ Upper: Trumpet 8', Flute 4', Quint, Nazard
  Lower: Diapason 8', Bassoon (or Reed) 8'
  Pedal: 16' + 8'
  Vibrato: Off

④ Upper: 00 3565 764
  Lower: (00)3344 430(0)
  Pedal: 5 – (3)
  Vibrato: Off

⑤ Upper: Flutes 16', 8', 2', + Sustain
  Lower: Orchestral Strings (or Strings 8', 4')
  Pedal: 16' + 8'
  Vibrato: Off. Leslie: Tremolo

⑤ Upper: 80 8000 008 + Sustain
  Lower: (00)5333 221(0)
  Pedal: 4 – (2)
  Vibrato: Off. Leslie: Tremolo

⑥ Upper: Brass Ensemble (or Trombone 16', Trumpet 8')
  Lower: Flutes 8', 4')
  Pedal: 16' + 8'
  Vibrato: On

⑥ Upper: 86 6555 000
  Lower: (00)8604 000(0)
  Pedal: 5 – (3)
  Vibrato: On

⑦ Upper: Orchestral Strings
  Lower: Flutes 8', 4'
  Pedal: 16' + 8'
  Vibrato: On

⑦ Upper: 00 5666 654
  Lower: (00)7504 000(0)
  Pedal: 5 – (3)
  Vibrato: On

⑧ Upper: Flutes 16', 8', 2', Piano
  Lower: Flute 8', String 8'
  Pedal: 16' + 8'
  Vibrato: Off. Leslie: Tremolo

⑧ Upper: 80 8006 008 + Piano
  Lower: (00)6544 333(0)
  Pedal: 5 – (3)
  Vibrato: Off. Leslie: Tremolo

1/95(19313)